Amazing Dogs

By Laura Buller

Series Editor Deborah Lock
Project Art Editor Hoa Luc
Art Director Martin Wilson
Producer, Pre-production Dragana Puvacic
Reading Consultant Jacqueline Harris

First published in Great Britain in 2016
by Dorling Kindersley Limited
80 Strand, London, WC2R 0RL

A CIP catalogue record for this book
is available from the British Library
ISBN: 978-0-2411-8688-6

Printed and bound in China.

The publisher would like to thank the following for
their kind permission to reproduce their photographs:
(Key: a-above; b-below/bottom; c-centre; f-far; l-left; r-right; t-top)
1 Corbis: Kennan Harvey / Aurora Open. 6 Alamy Images: Kathy Hancock.
7 Corbis: 2 / MGP / Ocean (b); Mark Edward Atkinson / Blend Images (tr).
8-9 Corbis: Denis Balibouse / Reuters. 10 Dreamstime.com: Ievgen Melamud / Elmmksat (t). 11
Corbis: DK Limited (br); Russell Glenister (tr); Yoshihisa Fujita / MottoPet / amanaimages (cla).
14 Corbis: Clive Chilvers / Demotix / Demotix / Demotix (cl). 14-15 Alamy Images: FEMA. 15
Alamy Images: Thorsten Eckert (tl). 18 Corbis: Renee DeMartin (cr). 18-19 Corbis: Tibor
Bognar / Photononstop. 19 Corbis: Radius Images (cr). 20 Alamy Images: Dave Porter (cl). 20-21
Corbis: Jack Affleck / Aurora Open. 22 Dreamstime.com: Engin Korkmaz / Hypnocreative.
23 Dreamstime.com: Roughcollie. 24-25 Corbis: 68 / Ocean. 26 Corbis: Robert Dowling. 27
Alamy Images: Guenter, B. / Juniors Bildarchiv GmbH. 28 Alamy Images: Huntstock / Disability
Images (bc). Corbis: Adie Bush / cultura (c). 29 Alamy Images: blickwinkel / Leithold (cr);
tbkmedia.de (bc). Getty Images: Fuse (tr). 30 Corbis: Julian Smith / epa. 31 Corbis: Ali Abbas /
epa (bl); Radius Images (tr). 32 Alamy Images: blickwinkel / Schmidt-Roeger (tr). 32-33 Corbis:
Penny Kendall / Design Pics. 33 Corbis: Kennan Harvey / Aurora Open (bl). 34 Corbis: Olivier
Maire / epa. 35 Corbis: Jean-Christophe Bott / epa (bl); Alan Carey (cra). 38 Corbis: Frederic
Larson / San Francisco Chronicle. 39 Corbis: Richard Hutchings. 40 Corbis: Brian Mitchell. 41
Corbis: Brian Mitchell (bl); Tom Nebbia (cra). 42 Alamy Images: AF archive (ca, c, bc).
Jacket images: Front: Corbis: Russell Glenister.Fotolia: fotojagodka (ca)
Back: Corbis: 2 / MGP / Ocean (tl)
All other images © Dorling Kindersley Limited
For further information see: www.dkimages.com

A WORLD OF IDEAS:
SEE ALL THERE IS TO KNOW
www.dk.com

Contents

Dogs from Small to Tall

Pekinese

Jack Russell terrier

Basset hound

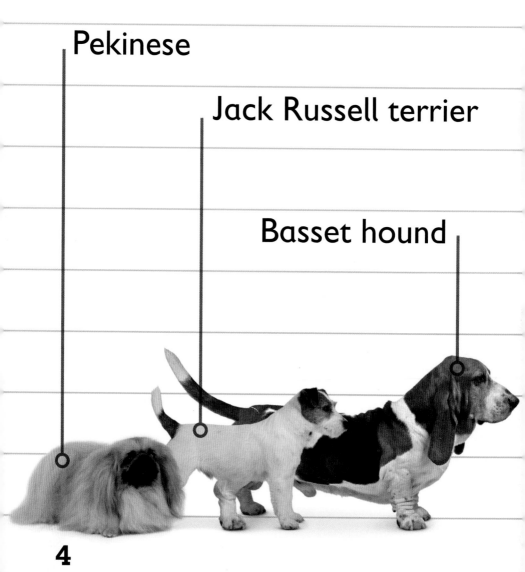

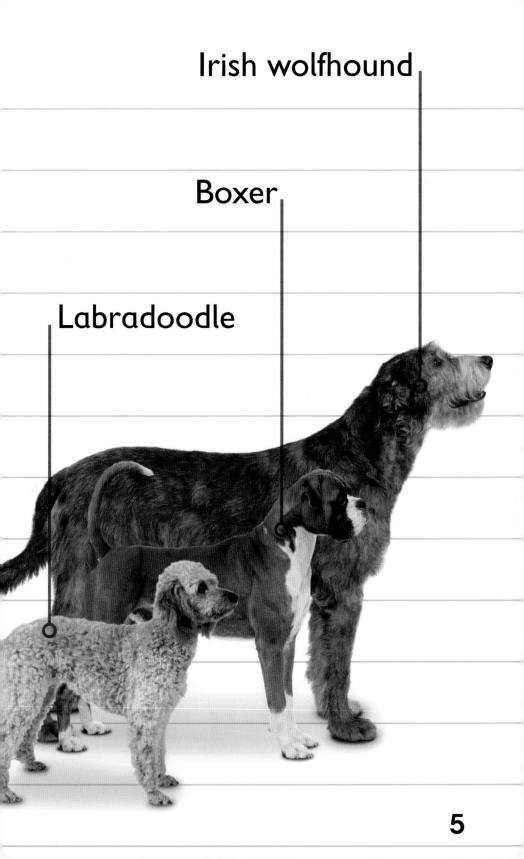

Irish wolfhound

Boxer

Labradoodle

5

CHAPTER 1
Hello, Doggy!

"Woof, woof!"

Dogs bark to say hello.

There are all kinds of dogs.
Some are so tiny
you can pick
them up for
a cuddle. Other
dogs are so big you
can hardly get your arms
around them for a hug!

Dogs belong to an animal
family called **mammals**.
They have fur, or hair,
like all mammals.
(You are
a mammal,
too!)

Baby dogs are called puppies. They drink milk from their mothers. Milk helps puppies grow bigger and stronger.

Puppy Games

Puppies
love to play.

They need to go
for walks and
run about.
This **exercise**
helps them grow.

  10

Puppies also play to learn.

They learn how to get along with other dogs.

CHAPTER 2
Super Senses

Dogs have super-strong **senses**. They can see better than you can — even in dim light.

They perk up their ears
to hear sounds –
even when you
think it is quiet.
But a dog's
real superpower
is its sense of smell.

Dogs have super senses
and skills. What can they do
with them? Plenty of things!

Some dogs are really amazing. They do some amazing jobs.

SUPERDOG!

He hears faraway sounds
that humans cannot!
Never fear, Superdog
will hear.

He sees faraway things
that you'd never spot!
Even a flea, Superdog sees.

His smelling is telling him
just what is what!
He follows his nose,
wherever he goes.
That's **SUPERDOG!**

CHAPTER 3

Round Up !

How do farmers keep their sheep safe? They depend on sheepdogs.

These dogs protect
the sheep from danger.
A sheepdog barks loudly
to scare away wild animals.
"Ruff! RUFF!"

How is a **herd** of **cattle** kept together? This is the job of a clever cattle dog.

This dog spots a cow stray from the herd. It nips the cow's ankle and the cow returns to the herd.

"Nip! Nip!"

Help Wanted!

Shepherd seeks a loyal and brave herding dog.

Do you know a dog that is fast on its feet and likes working in a team? Then this is the job for them!

The job:

- keeping bad animals away,

- obeying whistles to gather sheep,

- running at a calm and strong pace.

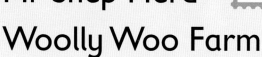

Apply to:

Mr Shep Herd
Woolly Woo Farm

Email: shep123@Woollywoofarm.com

CHAPTER 4
Pooch Power!

"Brrrrrrr!" It's freezing cold near the snowy **north pole**.

But this team of brave husky dogs get on with their job. They work together to pull a heavy **sledge**.

"Mush!" cries the driver, as the dogs pull and pull.

This mountain dog is big and strong. Farmers use dogs like this to help with the jobs.

They hitch the dog to a wooden cart. The cart is loaded with milk, cheese, fruits or vegetables. The dog pulls the cart to the market.

Home Help

How are these dogs being helpful?

CHAPTER 5
Dogs on Duty

"Sniff! Sniff!" These dogs are not being nosy. They are using their amazing sense of smell to help the police.

Police sniffer dogs
do all kinds of
useful work.

They can track down
runaway prisoners.

They can
sniff out
bad things
and sense
danger.

"Help!"
Someone is
in trouble.
Call in the
rescue dogs!

A person may get lost, stuck or in danger. A rescue dog uses its sniffing skills to find the person. Then rescue workers can get the person out of trouble.

The most famous rescue
dogs are Saint Bernard dogs.
They live in the snowy
Swiss Alps.

Climbers may get buried
in the snow. The dogs set off
to find them.
They dig
through
the snow.

Then they keep
people warm
until help
arrives.

Rescue Training

Search and rescue dogs are trained to find people using one or more of these skills.

Air scent dog:
picks up a person's
scent in the air.

Water search dog:
picks up a person's
scent in or under
the water.

Trailing dog: follows a person's scent close to the ground.

Tracking dog: follows a person's path.

Avalanche dog: picks up a person's scent in or under snow.

CHAPTER 6

Helping Hounds

Some people need a little extra help. There's a clever dog to help!

Dogs help people who are unable to see, hear or get around. These helpful dogs make jobs easier and safer for people.

Dogs can make people feel good. They are good friends for children with autism. Dogs make sick people cheerful. They are fun for lonely people.

Thank you, dogs, for all the amazing jobs you do!

FAMOUS DOGS

These dogs appear in books and films. They have amazing jobs, too!

Toto

Lassie

Rowlf

Amazing Dogs Quiz

1. Where do Saint Bernard dogs live?

2. What is a dog's best sense?

3. How do cattle dogs keep cows in the herd?

4. What does the driver of a sledge say to the husky dogs?

5. What animal family do dogs belong to?

Answers on page 45.

Glossary

cattle name for a group of cows

exercise activity that keeps a person or animal fit and healthy

herd group of animals that are the same

mammals group of animals, including humans, that have fur or hair, are warm-blooded and have backbones

north pole most northern place on Earth

rescue save someone from a dangerous place or situation

senses five senses are sight, smell, hearing, taste and touch

sledge small vehicle on runners for travel over snow or ice

Swiss Alps area of mountains that crosses many countries in central Europe, including Switzerland

Answers to the Amazing Dogs Quiz:
1. In the Swiss Alps; **2**. Its sense of smell; **3**. Dogs nip the cows on their ankles; **4**. Mush!; **5**. Dogs are mammals.

Guide for Parents

DK Readers is a four-level interactive reading adventure series for children, developing the habit of reading widely for both pleasure and information. These chapter books have an exciting main narrative interspersed with a range of reading genres to suit your child's reading ability. Each book is designed to develop your child's reading skills, fluency, grammar awareness, and comprehension in order to build confidence and engagement when reading.

Ready for a *Beginning to Read* book

YOUR CHILD SHOULD

- be using phonics, including consonant blends, such as bl, gl and sm, to read unfamiliar words; and common word endings, such as plurals, ing, ed and ly.

- be using the storyline, illustrations and the grammar of a sentence to check and correct his/her own reading.

- be pausing briefly at commas, and for longer at full stops; and altering his/her expression to respond to question, exclamation and speech marks.

A VALUABLE AND SHARED READING EXPERIENCE

For many children, reading requires much effort but adult participation can make this both fun and easier. So here are a few tips on how to use this book with your child.

TIP 1 Check out the contents together before your child begins:

- read the text about the book on the back cover.

- read through and discuss the contents page together to heighten your child's interest and expectation.

- make use of unfamiliar or difficult words on the page in a brief discussion.

- chat about the non-fiction reading features used in the book, such as headings, captions, recipes, lists or charts.

TIP 2 Support your child as he/she reads the story pages:

- give the book to your child to read and turn the pages.

- where necessary, encourage your child to break a word into syllables, sound out each one and then flow the syllables together. Ask him/her to reread the sentence to check the meaning.

- when there's a question mark or an exclamation mark, encourage your child to vary his/her voice as he/she reads the sentence. Demonstrate how to do this if it is helpful.

TIP 3 Praise, share and chat:

- the factual pages tend to be more difficult than the story pages, and are designed to be shared with your child.

- ask questions about the text and the meaning of the words used. These help to develop comprehension skills and awareness of the language used.

A FEW ADDITIONAL TIPS

- Try and read together everyday. Little and often is best. These books are divided into manageable chapters for one reading session. However after 10 minutes, only keep going if your child wants to read on.

- Always encourage your child to have a go at reading difficult words by themselves. Praise any self-corrections, for example, "I like the way you sounded out that word and then changed the way you said it, to make sense."

- Read other books of different types to your child just for enjoyment and information.

Index